I Mother

By

Zoe Hudson

I Mother Earth

A poetic journey through the elements
In remembrance of our relationship
With Mother Earth.

Dedicated to

My mother, daughters, grandchildren,

And Mother Earth

With love

Hear the Earth Calling

Hear the Earth calling,

For she is calling you,

She is calling me.

Her heart feels the collective heartbeat,

Of her beloved humanity.

She calls for a return back to her,

Through the spiral of eternity.

A call to come home back to her,

The natural place of well-being,

Of wholeness.

The home of humanity.

Contents

Foreword 2

Kind reflections 4

Appreciations 6

The Blue Jewel.................................... 8

Chapter 1: The Element of Water...................... 10

Chapter 2: The Element of Earth..................... 22

Chapter 3: The Element of Air..................... 36

Chapter 4: The Element of Fire........................ 42

Chapter 5: The Element of Space..................... 52

Chapter 6: Love.................................... 58

Chapter 7: Light.................................... 64

Foreword

I *Mother Earth* is written in the essence of poetic love and in devotion to the remembrance of our true nature with each other, with Mother Earth, the elements, and with the bigger cosmic picture.

It is a remembrance of our wholeness, our unity, and our oneness. The poems in this book take you on a journey through the elements, with a deep remembrance of the nature of the relationship that we enjoy with Mother Earth, the elements, and the cosmos.

These poems have been written with a commitment to keeping the golden, magical, light threads of poetry alive, which are woven within our hearts, our heavenly skies, in harmony with our beautiful Mother Earth's abundant waters and nature. Which make up the golden tapestry of our earthly existence.

This book has been created through years of deep journeying in well-being, creative expression and environmental art studies, alongside my deepening awareness of the role of the ancient wisdom of the Labyrinth in today's world.

The inner and outer landscapes of Somerset, Dorset, Devon, Cornwall, and Ireland have been the inspiration for these poems.

As we remember the way of the heart, the beauty in one another, and of the Earth, we remember a sense of place in harmony with ourselves, each other, and Mother Earth.

This remembrance can strengthen, nourish, and heal us, as we remember the true sense of place within our hearts, and the path home to the eternal sense of our divinity.

Zoe Hudson is a passionate environmental artist, poet, and well-being practitioner based in Devon, UK.

Kind reflections from friends

When Zoe communicates with us, she reminds us that we are all one. My own experience of her dance and poetry is that in harmony with her vision of service and with the dream of peace on earth.

Nancy Sherwood, grandmother, contemporary shaman, intuitive dancer, healer. Founder of The Moving Mandala and Traveller's Joy.

Zoe brings poetic imagination and love for Mother Earth together. These poems are moving and inspiring in the tradition of romantic poets. Zoe brings her love for Mother Earth together in a beautiful way.

Satish Kumar, editor emeritus *Resurgence & Ecologist* magazine.

Zoe's reading of her poems, inspired by each of the elements, was a magical experience that brought me deep into peace.
I felt a beautiful, weaving of strands of light, of energy, taking us step by step into the One Heart. It was the experience of the walk to the centre of the labyrinth, the pattern of our journey of remembering back to the Heart of Love.

Felicity Paton

Appreciations

Appreciation with love for our Mother Earth, the planet we all call home, and for all humanity, especially the children and all beings.

Eternal love and appreciation for my partner Ben, for his loving presence, wisdom, cover photography, and support alongside me on this journey of life and in the creation of this book.

Eternal love and appreciation for my inspirational and beautiful daughters of change, Jade, Heidi, and Jenna, and also for their partners, who love and support them. They each bring so much love, meaning, and presence to my life, full of sparkle and deep wisdom. It is because of my love for them and for the earth that this book was created.

Eternal love and appreciation for my dear grandchildren, their love, presence, and their joy inspire me.

Eternal love and appreciation for my dear Mum and Dad, who love and support me.

Heart appreciation for Sue-Claire Morris, for walking the shamanic labyrinth path with me, as a soul sister, and for her support as a former teacher in the Environmental Arts.

Heart appreciation for Nancy Sherwood, for being my shamanic teacher for some years, and for being a soul sister along the way. Her support of my process will always be remembered with love.

Heart appreciation for my Travellers Joy, Moving Mandala *Sis stars* Nancy, Sue-Claire, Lori, Margot, Brenda, Ali, and Tina for all the transformative spaces we have all shared together over the years.

Heart appreciation for Satish Kumar, a wise elder who has supported my poetry and the environmental art programme

that Sue-Claire and I developed. Appreciation for the poem he shared with me to help me keep going, with the mantra *Ekla Chalo Re*, a poem written by Rabindranath Tagore.

Heart appreciation for Lauren Artress, Founder of Veriditas.

Heartfelt appreciation for all my beautiful family and friends in my life, including Lyn and Graham Whiteman, Kim Dewey, Jo Smith Oliver, and for all those whom I have not mentioned, with love and a thank you for the support along the way. I am truly appreciative and blessed to share the path with you all.

The Blue Jewel

The Blue Jewel Star, sparkling, from where I am seeing

From another far-off distant galaxy.

In I dive, through the oceans of consciousness.

Diving into the oceans of this earth,

In search of the sacred pearl within thee,

I reach the surface of the universal waters.

Chapter 1

Water

Ancient water of the Earth, and of my body.

Great Mother, your presence surrounds me,

In the energy of your waters.

Ocean Mother, vast multitude of cosmic oceans,

Merge as one.

Angel of Water

Angel of Water,

Filtering the elixir of my higher self,

Through my crown.

Angel of Water,

I give thanks to thee.

I ask to cleanse,

And prepare my water body,

With the frequencies that my DNA sees.

I reach the surface of the Universal Waters

From the light,

Deeply embedded within my soul,

I feel the spark of life,

Illuminate my body.

I feel my bones within my awakening,

Move with every breath I take.

I reach the surface of the universal waters,

Gasp and breathe.

I am here in body,

Here in union with the earth,

Here in union with peace,

Here in union with love.

Cosmic molecules that I remember I am made of

Here, after travelling light years

To be here now.

Deeply diving in to my Mother's Waters

Eternal Ocean of Love,

Caressing my soul for aeons,

Forever whispering memories back to me,

Through my soul.

I feel the vibration of your love, dear Mother.

All-encompassing,

Divine Mother's love,

Soothing my heart.

My heart fills like a well,

Overflowing with love.

My heart, like a delicate flower,

Neither human or of matter,

Divine, delicate heart of tenderness.

Heart of tender love,

Cosmic tender light,

Deeply diving in to my mother's waters.

Well of Promise

Walking footsteps of light,

Awakening the garden,
Awakening me as an eternal one.

Journeying along,

With the sacred ever-beloved one.
Well of promise, well of old,

Opens revealing its ancient timeless energy.

A portal of luminescence,
Deep chasms,

Deep tunnels,

Linking the web of light.

Radiant starlight,

Forming into the water.

Be at peace my dear daughter,

Be at peace my dear son,

For you are children of the light.

Look deeper into the water.
A reflection you see,

Within my waters,

For is it you dear Mother,

Or is it me, your dear daughter?

Divine love for my dear Mother.

Crowned together,

Crowned with stars,

Crowned in unity.

May your crown of light be forever yours,

A crown of light, in love, a crown of peace.

In honour of our dear Mother, who holds us all in her
natural rhythm.

For she holds a key for us all.
May we hold her too, with deep love, deep honour,

In eternal deep peace.

Written at
The Chalice Well
Glastonbury.

Sacred water

Water rushing,

Eternal pouring,

Opening my heart,

No more ignoring.

Open the gate.

Cleansing waters come forth.

Water, rushing, pouring,

Opening my heart,

No more ignoring.

Sacred water,

So pure, so clear,

Awaken intentions,

Within my heart so dear.

Cleanse my heart,

Cleanse my soul,

Cleanse me until I remember ancient wisdom of old.

Water, rushing, pouring,

Opening of my heart,

No more ignoring.

Energy flowing,

Energy washing,

Energy clearing.

Reawaken,

Reawaken,

Awake now,

For the time is coming.

Beautiful Water

Dance with me on the edge of the shore,

Silvery moonlight lighting us up.

Amazement of life,

Emotion of the water that replicates.

Flow with the feeling,

That it's not too late.

Pay attention to the water's subtle vibrations,

For then we can open the gate.

A gate to the deeper soul knowing,

Of the water's wisdom.

Look closely within,

For it is already showing.

Water

Water so clear,

Essence of blue swirling,

The eternal bliss,

Within and without.

Eternal in presence,

Deeply known for all time.

So treasured, so precious,

Your voice becomes clearer.

Speaking so clearly,

In a language all of your own.

Your language unique,

So innocent and pure.

I will listen to your voice forever,

Your divine wisdom,

The essence of my divine Mother,

Forever . . .

River

River, you flow to the sea.
River, remember,
It's you and it's me.
Engaged and connected.

As your secrets unfolded,
Before once upon a time,
When water was honoured,
Blessed and cared for.

How I long for those times again.
Thanks always given for each time it was taken,
I plead now in the remembrance of our divine connection,
With all water, rivers, seas and oceans.

Flowing River

Flowing river of eternal tides.

Sacred Moon,

Iridescent reflections.

Deepening, Soothing,

Are the tides of direction,

Within the flowing river of the eternal.

Chapter 2

The Element of Earth

Summertime was the season,
Where I walked barefoot
Upon the green grass of Dartmoor.
Moss akin to an emerald essence.
So soft, so inviting.

As I lay my head down.
For it was then that I heard my mother, as she spoke:
"I Mother Earth, I speak for all to feel me in their hearts."

Angel of Earth

Angel of Earth,

My earthly body responds to you.

The clay of my existence

Resides with heart gratitude for you,

Dear Angel of Earth,

Who supports my re-birth.

Mother Earth's Soul

Touching gently my belly,

My navel, upon your body.

Held with eternal love,

And deeply supported.

Held as if suspended

Upon the star of this universe,

Our Blue Jewel.

Radiant, divine star,

Shining pearl of blue,

With hues of pearlescent white,

Soothing my soul.

Dear Mother Divine,

I feel your body,

So close to mine.

Divine soul eternal,

Mother Earth divine.

Sacred Earth

Sacred earth,

Our home, our hearth, our shelter,

Our food, our warmth.

Our Mother who cares for all our needs and more.

For she holds space for us all to co-create,

No matter how big,

No matter how small.

Her journey is to carry herself, us all, to higher places.

Look deep within each other's eyes.

Look deep within.

For you will remember each other's faces . . .

Written in Beaminster, Dorset.

My bare feet touch the Earth

My bare feet touch the Earth.

The subtle vibrations connecting my heart,

With the heart of the Earth, My Mother.

My energetic roots reach into my Mother's Sacred Heart.

Our close bond deepens,

Deeper and deeper.

Meeting each other in our hearts,

The sacred place of oneness.

Where everything is held,

Suspended as if in space.

A space as large as this Universe,

Yet so tiny in its form.

My Mother's energy entwined with mine,

Dancing, pulsing, radiating.

Lovingly entwined heavenly light.

Ancient connections in love, in honour,

In honour of our beautiful connection,

In love and in honour of our dear Mother Earth.

Hear my prayers,

The appreciation in the deepening,

As you soothe my soul.

Your loving aura wraps around me,

Your eternal love radiates through me.

So familiar is this love that I feel,

As the soles of my bare feet,

Touch your sacred Earth.

Dear Mother,

My love for you

Is as ancient as is your love for me.

I Mother Earth

I Mother Earth.

I speak for all to feel me in their hearts.

Aeons of time have passed,

Time is nigh to share my message.

I am the vessel that carries humanity,

Humanity also within thee.

Balancing sacred femininity,

Balancing sacred masculinity.

Abundance of beauty, love, peace, healing,

And food for all to see.

Harmony creating heart-centred community,

One heart, one love, one way.

The blood in my veins, you know as your rivers,

Which flow into oceans.

Oh, such sacred waters,

For you are made of these,

My dear sons, my dear daughters.

Remember, remember, please,

My love for you all is for eternity.

My ancient heartbeat, in rhythm with yours,

Such heartbeat, forever strong.

Singing the divine eternal love song,

For love is the golden key,

Awakening all of humanity.

Awaken, awaken to our true essence,

We are one with our Mother Earth.

A larger part of ourselves,

For she is you, see.

Honour, love, care for ourselves, each other,

Our Mother,

Our pure divinity.

For in this energy, we will all find our way home.

You, she, he, and me.

All will be nourished,

All will be fed,

All will be loved.

No more fear,

No more dread.

Sacred days, sacred nights.

As we lie in our beds awakening from our slumber,

Our hearts, our eyes, now open,

For by our hearts, we are now led.

One heart, one love, one way.

Gather your wisdom to share,

Come together as one,

As it is inevitable that this time has come.

A NEW WORLD,

A new world,

A new way.

Mother Nature's love, for all to share,

Full of laughter, song, dancing into play.

For our joy will light the way.

As old ways dissolve,

New ways flower,

Increasingly unfolding,

Silently evolving.

Ancient wisdom,

Co-creating with the now,

Is here for us all.

No-one to be left behind.

So, gather,

Join hands,

Stand tall.

Step into the peace,

Walk upon me in bare feet.

Feel me speak from my heart to yours.

Feel me in the wind,

Encouraging your hearts to sing.

Feel me in the Earth,

Nurturing your seeds of dreams.

Feel me cleanse your mind, your body, your soul.

As you immerse yourselves,

Within my ancient oceans of old.

Feel me in our Father Sun,

Sparking the creative fire in everyone.

Come dance with me,

For I am here always,

Waiting for you.

Come, share with me,

For it is never a moment too soon . . .

Written on Dartmoor, Devon.

I am the World Peace Tree

Hold on dear child,

For there is no need to weep,

For I speak, I speak, I speak.

In your vision, in your dream,

Awake, and when you sleep.

Anchored deep within our Mother Earth,

Come home children, to my hearth.

Remember, that you are a part of this infinite universe.

Branches gently caressing,

Healing, healing, healing.

Reaching, reaching, reaching,

To touch your beautiful skin.

Hear me speak dear child,

For there is no need to weep.

I am the source of your breath,

I am with you beyond any forms of death.

My ancient roots reaching, reaching,

Down in to the depths of our mother earth.

Twisting, twisting, twisting,

Turning to her centre core.

Pulsating, regenerating, illuminating.

Back up through my roots,

Twisting, turning,

Yearning, yearning, yearning.

For I am strong,

Yet delicate you see,

I dear child am,

The world peace tree.

Symbolising a woven, energetic, destiny.

A returning to the standing people.

Gentle yet strong,

Quiet yet profound.

Indicating how well our Mother Earth feels,

A true reflection of how she sounds.

Come dear child,

For solace, love, peace,

Come now for healing.

For the rainbow tribe gather,

Grandfathers, grandmothers,

Mothers, fathers,

Sons and daughters.

I, as the tree,

Ask you all to come, and be with me.

Find love, peace, healing, journey into the dance,

Eternally with me,

The Universal World Peace Tree.

Together we remember our true purpose.

Together we remember our true divinity.

Together we remember our true destiny . . .

Written in

Knowle Woods

East Devon.

Chapter 3

Air

Walking through the door,

Immediate swiftness,

To dancing on air.

Streams of energy,

Sparkling, white silver light,

Radiating from my body, hands, and feet.

Dancing the light,

Singing and speaking the light.

Creating vortexes with Mother Earth.

Angel of Air

Angel of Air

Brings conscious breath to my sacred body.

Swirling, moving,

Through the chambers of my heart.

Fuelling my sacred body,

I give thanks.

Angel of Air,

Support my flight,

As I embrace and accept my wings.

Sacred Air

Sacred air,

Sweet divine essence,

Which carries our prayers.

In the winds of change,

In the winds of love,

In the safe flight,

Of the pure white dove.

Flowing, flowing, flowing,

Prayers carry momentum.

Prayers that carry intention.

Prayers of love and hope.

Peace is the totem.

Growing, growing, growing.

In the winds of change,

In the winds of love,

In the safe flight of the pure white dove.

Translucent, transparent, transcendent, light air.

Dancing, swiftly caressing, silently changing,

Divine clear air.

In the winds of change,

On the wings of love,

For we are now in the safe flight,

Of the pure white dove . . .

Feathers of Peace

Feathers of Peace,
Uniting all of us.
Feathers of peace,
Bathing all of us.

The weight of the feather,
So light, for it lifts all of us.
Lifts us up on to a stream of effortless flow.
Surrender, release,
Let go, let go, let go.

Feeling lighter than air now,
Expansive clear skies so blue.
Space to be, space to fly,
Space to be me, space to be you.

Our vibrations now as light as a feather.
Our new wings carry us forth,
In the direction of the new dawn.
Waiting for all the winged ones to gather,
In the heavenly God, Goddess, sky hall.

Feathers of peace.
Feathers of peace.
Feathers of peace ...

Chapter 4

Fire

In the innermost glow,

Within the hearth of the heart,

The embers of an eternal flame flicker.

The warmth of this flame warms the soul,

Wraps one into the essence of the eternal source flow.

Angel of fire

Angel of fire,

Sacred holy fire,

Fuelling the co-creator within.

Angel of fire,

Support my flame,

As I rise to become more,

Of the person I am here to be.

The Holy Fire

The Holy Fire,
Great source of light burning,
Yet gentle love from the divine.

Within our hearts,
We feel the spark.
The flame ignited,
Deep within our hearts.

Something deep inside remembered.
Something deep inside realised.
Our hearts feel joy,
As the flame within is realised.

Our hearts feel joy,
As the flame within is nurtured.
Memories of peace,
Coming forwards to the now.

Alongside the awakening of our creative souls.

Knowing we are the co-creators we have been waiting for.
As we tend to the Holy Flame that resides

Within all our hearts . . .

Written in England.

Capturing the essence of

The Festival of the Fires of Ireland.

Sacred Fire

Sacred Fire,
Heaven sent.
Purify, purify, purify.
Golden white flame,
Alight forever.

You and I, you and I, you and I.
Dancing, flickering, burning,
Transcendent into the divine.
Illuminating your heart,
Illuminating mine.

Golden white light,
Energising the soul,
Cleansing the heart,
Purifying the mind.

Dance, dance, dance,
Rise from the flame.

Spread your wings.

An eternal phoenix,

Whose prayers have been heard.

Fly, fly, fly,

Beyond limitations,

Into the light,

Bringing your eternal flame into being.

A transcendent,

Pure, divine, white gold light.

Here gathered in this circle

Here gathered in this circle,

Gathered in honour of our divine Mother,

In honour of our divine Father,

In honour of the divine within each other.

The essence of divine light.

The holy fire that we are.

Carrying hope within our hearts.

Sharing truth from our hearts.

Many paths we have travelled,

To arrive here today.

Old friends re-gather,

Why are we here?

And why are we together?

Close your eyes,

Feel into the love that you are.

Feel at one with me, your mother.

Feel at one with me, your father.

48

Held tenderly as a child.

Pure divine love,

Pure divine light.

As the light becomes brighter,

We merge like fluid.

Dancing together,

As we become one.

Written at the Chalice well gardens,

Glastonbury UK.

The Well

You are the place for all to heal,

Time fades away, within the waters of this well.

For looking deep into the well,

I see reflections of the past,

Of the present,

And of the future.

Archangels Michael, Raphael, and Gabriel,

Guard this sacred place eternally,

Keepers of the sacred well.

Written at the Chalice well gardens,

Glastonbury UK.

Chapter 5

Space

Through the crack in the very existence of all space,

There dwells a place of verdant contraction.

Breathing with the expansion.

Angel of Space

Angel of space,

Kindly show me more,

Of the alchemy,

Of the space within the heart.

Angel of space,

Share with me,

The space of expansion,

Yet sacred,

And tiny.

The Silent Space

Thank you, Source, for space.

Thank you for the expansive space to breathe.

To breathe, in-between the chapters of life.

As we, when ready, prepare to shift.

We enter a void of silence,

The silent space,

The place of nowhere,

Yet everywhere.

Sacred Space

Sacred space,

Apparent empty,

Clear, space.

The void.

The sacred space,

Space to be held,

Space of surrender,

Space of release,

Space given to trust within.

A sacred place,

For us all to remember.

We are held,

We are supported.

Surrender,

Surrender,

Surrender.

For you are carried, dear ones,

Within this sacred space.

Carried safely,

Through the vast silver vibration of space.

A place of ancient wisdom,

Yet nothing can be seen with thy human eyes.

Yet within your hearts you see.

Deep within knowing,

That all is very well.

Before long,

New horizons are felt within your heart.

For it is then you begin to clearly see,

That Space is a sacred place,

Which invites us all to remember.

Dream space

Dreams these days are becoming seamless.

Merging into the remembrance of the oneness.

Entering Dream space.

Chapter 6

Love is

Beings of light,

Of energy.

That which you are,

Is love.

The Universal Sacred Heart

Stored within the sacred heart of heaven,

Are all the tools known to humankind.

Open your heart,

Remember who you truly are.

So radiantly bright, as a shining star.

Climbing new altitudes,

New heights.

Beyond all comprehension.

Release and let go,

Of all density,

Of life's apparent tensions.

For now, is the time.

Breathe deep and allow,

All wisdom to flow,

Through the channels of the rivers within.

Release and let go,

Of all expectation.

Realising there is no separation.

As we all collectively remember,

The universal sacred hearts connection.

Eternal cosmic love

Eternal cosmic love,

Showering golden love.

Pale golden white,

Full of divine spark.

Shimmering hues of pink, golden, white light.

Radiating, illuminating, vibrating.

Blossoms of petals,

From the rose of love.

Sweet flower of the divine,

Growing within your heart and mine.

Intense heartbeat of this cosmic love,

Which holds together this planet,

This Universe,

And all others.

This fragrance of cosmic love,

Which travels across the illusion of time.

Travels across wide astral oceans,

Within infinite skies.

Cosmic love,

Swirling,

Dancing,

Spiralling.

Coming into our orbit,

Upon the wings of the Cosmic swan.

Pure,

Divine,

Cosmic love.

As the Stars align

As the stars align,

An ever-flowing source of light streams forth,

Illuminating all hearts,

Into the light of the cosmic heart,

Of the cosmic love.

That exists from the beginning,

And that holds everything together,

Forever.

Chapter 7

The Light

Walking footsteps of light,

Through dimensions.

Paths of light, weaving starlight.

Silver starlight, merges with golden starlight.

Becoming white gold light, together as one.

The time is upon us to remember,

The eternal light,

That shines within all our hearts.

Poems inspired by the inner flame and outer dance of the heart
mostly written in the landscape of Glastonbury, UK.

The Children of the Sun are here

The children of the sun are here,

With the children of the earth.

Our ancestors surround us.

Our angels walk with us.

Our divine Mother embraces us.

Our divine Father loves us.

We feel their love in our hearts,

They feel our love for them.

Within their hearts.

We are divine love,

Our divine light,

Our wholeness,

Our whole being shines.

Our radiant divine light,

Shines upon the pathway,

Of the new dawn.

Shine, shine, shine.

Embrace the light.

Immerse yourself fully,

Within the light.

Merge like golden fluid,

For we are the light.

Brightly shining

Rays of gold,

Radiating in all directions.

Celebrating the sacred turning of the wheel.

For we are all on this journey,

Remembering to heal.

Remembering our wholeness,

We merge like fluid,

For we are the light, radiating

Love, truth, peace.

For in this vibration,

We can be at ease.

Being within divine truth.

Beings of light,

Of energy.

That which you are,

Is love.

The Portal of Luminescence

Deep chasms that dwell inside of your heart,

Depths within linking you to the web of light.

Radiant starlight,

Shining Into the portal of luminescence.

Deep within your Soul

White gold alchemy,

Spinning circles of divine eternity.

Light-filled molecules of ancient codes,

Deep within your soul.

Illuminating radiance of light dear one,

That which you are.

Eternal Emerald Oceans of Light

Through the eternal emerald oceans of light,
I come forth through the portal,
With the truth, of the love, and of the light.

Emerald rays soaking the earth.
Honouring of the divine feminine,
Alongside her divine masculine.
Awakening the sovereign within.

Honouring of the here,
The place where the heart can be,
To radiate amongst the stars within.
The emerald glow of the divine self-realised.

Emerald Veil

Through the emerald veil,

Swimming through the astral emerald ocean.

Fill your body with the elixir of your soul.

Remember your soul, remember you.

Dressing in your emerald star body,

In the silence.

The Light

Shine, shine, shine,

Embrace the light.

Immerse yourselves fully within the light.

Merge like fluid,

For we are the light.

Rays of gold radiating in all directions.

Merge like fluid,

For we are the light.

Radiating love, truth and peace.

For in this vibration, we can be at ease.

Being divine light.

Shine, shine, shine.

Embrace the light.

Immerse yourselves fully within the light.

Feel the immense love of our ever-present, radiant sun,

Shining within and upon us all.

So, shine in your beauty,

Pure divine energy.

Remember

You are the light,

You are the love.

You are the peace.

The Sacred Pearl

Our journey into the descent of the darkness,

Of the vast void of space is nearly complete.

The journey into the sacred space of the heart,

Passing through the darkness of space.

Journeying with our shadows,

A time for transformation.

Now is the moment for rebirth,

For within the darkness,

That has now come to pass,

The divine flame within the flower of our hearts

Is remembered.

The journey into our hearts,

There revealed is the divine flame of love,

Burning gently.

Eternal white-gold flame.

This flame is the keeper of the sacred pearl within.

The sacred pearl,

Keeper of all that was,

All that is,

And all of what is to be.

Honour the sacred pearl within your heart.
Let it guide you always,

To all that ever was, is,

And to all that is yet to be....

Printed in Great Britain
by Amazon

79978053R00047